Momentous Materials
Plastic

by Trudy Becker

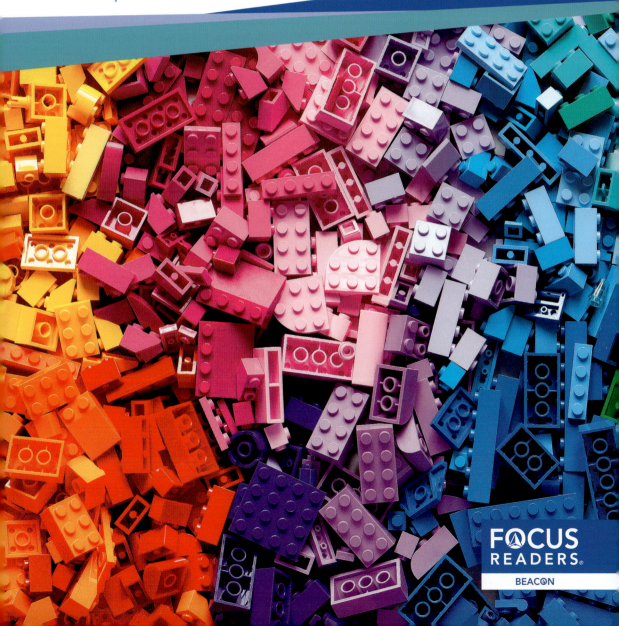

www.focusreaders.com

Copyright © 2024 by Focus Readers®, Mendota Heights, MN 55120. All rights reserved. No part of this book may be reproduced or utilized in any form or by any means without written permission from the publisher.

Focus Readers is distributed by North Star Editions:
sales@northstareditions.com | 888-417-0195

Produced for Focus Readers by Red Line Editorial.

Photographs ©: Shutterstock Images, cover, 1, 4, 7, 8, 10, 13, 14, 16, 18, 20–21, 22, 24, 27, 29

Library of Congress Cataloging-in-Publication Data
Names: Becker, Trudy, author.
Title: Plastic / Trudy Becker.
Description: Mendota Heights, MN : Focus Readers, [2024] | Series: Momentous materials | Includes bibliographical references and index. | Audience: Grades 2-3
Identifiers: LCCN 2023028115 (print) | LCCN 2023028116 (ebook) | ISBN 9798889980346 (hardcover) | ISBN 9798889980773 (paperback) | ISBN 9798889981596 (ebook pdf) | ISBN 9798889981206 (hosted ebook)
Subjects: LCSH: Plastics--Juvenile literature. | Plastic scrap--Environmental aspects--Juvenile literature. | Recycling industry--Juvenile literature.
Classification: LCC TP1125 .B425 2024 (print) | LCC TP1125 (ebook) | DDC 668.4--dc23/eng/20230701
LC record available at https://lccn.loc.gov/2023028115
LC ebook record available at https://lccn.loc.gov/2023028116

Printed in the United States of America
Mankato, MN
012024

About the Author

Trudy Becker lives in Minneapolis, Minnesota. She likes exploring new places and loves anything involving books.

Table of Contents

CHAPTER 1

Melt and Shape 5

CHAPTER 2

History of Plastic 9

CHAPTER 3

Modern Methods 15

THAT'S AMAZING!

Biodegradable Plastic 20

CHAPTER 4

Many Uses, Many Problems 23

Focus on Plastic • 28
Glossary • 30
To Learn More • 31
Index • 32

Chapter 1

Melt and Shape

Machines spin and clank inside a factory. The machines are working with a hot liquid. When the liquid is ready, the plastic mixture is poured into a **mold**. The mixture hardens into a tube shape.

Making plastic involves many steps.

Next, workers send the plastic tubes to a different factory. There, the tubes are heated again. They are filled with air. They form the shape of bottles.

Soon, the bottles cool. They are taken out of the mold. Now they are ready for use. Workers send the bottles to drink companies. These

Did You Know?

People use more than one billion plastic bottles every day.

 Most plastic bottles end up in landfills rather than being recycled.

companies fill the bottles. Then they label them. Finally, the bottles go to stores. People can buy them. The plastic has come a long way.

Chapter 2

History of Plastic

Plastics are materials that can be molded and shaped. Before the invention of plastic, people used similar materials from nature. Animal horns are one example. Horns can be melted.

Long ago, people made horns into cups for drinking.

9

 Ivory comes from elephants' tusks. Many places have laws against buying and selling ivory.

Then they can be reshaped. People also used **shellac** from beetles.

By the late 1800s, people had killed many elephants for ivory. Also, it took a long time to get enough shellac from beetles. And these materials were not cheap. People needed human-made replacements. Some groups held contests. Inventors worked on making new materials.

One new material was called Bakelite. It was created in 1907.

In 1869, John Wesley Hyatt entered a contest. He made a synthetic ivory. Hyatt won. But he never collected the $10,000 reward.

The inventor said it had many uses. He was right. Bakelite became a huge success. It was used in cars, jewelry, washing machines, and much more.

Other new types of plastic soon followed. Examples included nylon and plexiglass. The new plastics were strong, light, and cheap. Also, making **single-use** items was easy. For these reasons, production grew quickly. Plastic-making tripled during World War II (1939–1945).

 By the 2020s, half of all plastic products were single-use items.

When the war ended, plastic production kept growing. The material had become part of most people's lives. However, a new worry came up. Scientists noticed that plastic harmed the environment.

Chapter 3

Modern Methods

There are many kinds of plastic. So, there are many ways to create it. Most plastics are made from **fossil fuels** such as oil. Factories heat these fuels. That causes materials in the fuels to separate.

 Factories that make products out of oil are called refineries.

 Workers at plastic factories can develop health problems because of the dangerous chemicals.

After that, factories can create polymers. Polymers are materials with long, repeating units. They are light, strong, and flexible.

Next, factories can mix different chemicals into the polymers.

Some chemicals change the color of the plastic. Some make the plastic stronger. And some make it more flexible.

Next, the plastic goes into a tank. The tank heats the plastic. After that, it can be molded into a shape. Finally, the plastic cools.

In the past, these processes were difficult. But now, advanced machines help. Plastic production happens much more quickly. Large amounts can be made at once.

 Plastic pollution is a major problem in many places around the world.

Plastic can be very useful. Yet it also causes major problems. Creating plastic from fossil fuels harms the planet. Large amounts of energy are used. That causes **greenhouse gases** to go into the air. These gases are causing **climate change**.

People have tried to recycle more plastic. But scientists warn that recycling isn't enough. They say people need to produce less plastic. Less-harmful production methods are needed, too.

Did You Know?

Certain plastics can be melted down and used again. That makes them easier to recycle.

THAT'S AMAZING!

Biodegradable Plastics

Plastics take a long time to break down. That can be useful. It helps products last. But many plastic products are single-use. So, people throw them away. Then, the plastic sits in landfills. It takes hundreds or thousands of years to break down.

Some inventors are creating **biodegradable** plastics instead. These plastics break down more easily. One example is plastic from corn. It takes less energy to make. It has fewer harmful effects. And it can break down in just months.

Some grocery stores have biodegradable bags.

Chapter 4

Many Uses, Many Problems

For most people, it would be hard to go a single day without using plastic. That's because most clothing is made with plastic. Tiny pieces of plastic are part of the fabric.

Many clothes include a blend of plastic and cotton.

23

 Plastic is hard to avoid in the modern world.

These microplastics can help the clothes last longer. However, some microplastics break away when clothes are washed. They go down the drain. Then they get into rivers and oceans. There, microplastics harm wildlife. They can even get into humans' food supply.

Many items come wrapped in plastic **packaging**. Plastic is also in kitchen items and furniture. It's in toys and electronics. Almost every part of daily life involves plastic.

Fixing this problem is difficult. That's partly because plastic use is so widespread. But scientists warn that something must change.

Reducing plastic production would help. So would cleaner methods of making it. New laws could help, too.

Lawmakers are making some progress. For example, countries in Europe proposed new laws about plastic in 2022. Those laws would reduce packaging waste. Enough

Did You Know?

By the early 2020s, several US states had laws about single-use plastic. However, there was no national law.

 Many people use reusable shopping bags instead of single-use plastic bags.

actions like these could bring a positive change to the world of plastic.

FOCUS ON
Plastic

Write your answers on a separate piece of paper.

1. Write a few sentences explaining the main ideas of Chapter 4.

2. Do you think your area is doing enough to reduce plastic waste? Why or why not?

3. When was Bakelite invented?
   - **A.** early 1800s
   - **B.** early 1900s
   - **C.** early 2000s

4. How can plastics get into the food supply?
   - **A.** When plastic is recycled, it is mixed with plants that people eat.
   - **B.** Bits of plastic break off of farmers' tractors and end up in crops.
   - **C.** Fish eat microplastics in oceans, and then people eat those fish.

5. What does **replacements** mean in this book?

*People needed human-made **replacements**. Some groups held contests. Inventors worked on making new materials.*

    A. people who come up with new ideas
    B. new items to use in place of old ones
    C. events that people try to win

6. What does **proposed** mean in this book?

*For example, countries in Europe **proposed** new laws about plastic in 2022. Those laws would reduce packaging waste.*

    A. invented a new type of material
    B. came up with ideas for something
    C. stopped throwing things away

Answer key on page 32.

Glossary

biodegradable
Able to be broken down into harmless materials.

climate change
A human-caused global crisis involving long-term changes in Earth's temperature and weather patterns.

fossil fuels
Energy sources that come from the remains of plants and animals that died long ago.

greenhouse gases
Gases that trap heat in Earth's atmosphere, causing climate change.

mold
An empty container that is filled with hot liquid. The liquid takes a specific shape when it cools and hardens.

packaging
The material that covers an item before someone buys it.

shellac
A material from insects. It can be used to make hard, shiny coatings.

single-use
Made to be used once and then thrown away.

synthetic
Made by people, not by nature.

To Learn More

BOOKS

Crull, Kelly. *Washed Ashore: Making Art from Ocean Plastic*. Minneapolis: Lerner Publishing, 2022.

Forest, Christopher. *Fossil Fuels*. Minneapolis: Abdo Publishing, 2020.

Owen, Ruth. *The Problem with Plastic: Know Your Facts, Take Action, Save the Oceans*. Minneapolis: Ruby Tuesday Books, 2021.

NOTE TO EDUCATORS

Visit **www.focusreaders.com** to find lesson plans, activities, links, and other resources related to this title.

Index

B
Bakelite, 11–12
biodegradable plastics, 20
bottles, 6–7

C
climate change, 19
clothing, 23–24

F
fossil fuels, 15, 18

H
horns, 9

I
ivory, 10–11

L
laws, 26

M
microplastics, 24–25
molds, 5–6

N
nylon, 12

P
packaging, 25–26
plexiglass, 12
polymers, 16

R
recycling, 19

S
shellac, 10–11
single-use items, 12, 20, 26

Answer Key: **1.** Answers will vary; **2.** Answers will vary; **3.** B; **4.** C; **5.** B; **6.** B